T0276952

THE
MAGIC
PATH OF
INTUITION

Also by
Florence Scovel Shinn

The Game of Life and How to Play It*

Your Word Is Your Wand

The Secret Door to Success

The Power of the Spoken Word

*Available from Hay House

Please visit:

Hay House USA: www.hayhouse.com®
Hay House Australia: www.hayhouse.com.au
Hay House UK: www.hayhouse.co.uk
Hay House India: www.hayhouse.co.in

THE
MAGIC
PATH OF
INTUITION

Florence Scovel Shinn

HAY HOUSE, INC.
Carlsbad, California • New York City
London • Sydney • New Delhi

Published in the United States by: Hay House, Inc.: www
.hayhouse.com® • *Published in Australia by:* Hay House Australia Pty. Ltd.: www.hayhouse.com.au • *Published in the
United Kingdom by:* Hay House UK, Ltd.: www.hayhouse
.co.uk • *Published in India by:* Hay House Publishers India:
www.hayhouse.co.in

Cover and interior design: Tricia Breidenthal

Library of Congress Control Number: 2013936893

Hardcover ISBN: 978-1-4019-4415-5
E-book ISBN: 978-1-4019-4467-4

24 23 22 21 20 19 18 17 16 15
1st edition, December 2013

Printed in the United States of America

This product uses responsibly sourced papers and/or recycled
materials. For more information, see www.hayhouse.com.

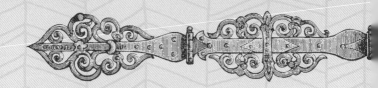

CONTENTS

★ INTRODUCTION ★

In 1925 Florence Scovel Shinn made her debut on the metaphysical scene with her first book, *The Game of Life and How to Play It.* Not long after this, I was born.

Although Ms. Shinn died in 1940, I have long felt a kinship with her. I first came across her work in 1972 as I was beginning my own exploration of the metaphysical world, and I have been enamored of her ever since. I resonated with her no-nonsense way of writing—her words spoke to me, and I became a devoted follower. I often quoted her affirmations and shared them with my own students.

The years passed. Then, in the fall of 2012, a rare-books dealer found a small, typewritten unpublished manuscript of the last writings of Florence Scovel Shinn. Here is an excerpt from the letter that was sent with it:

Several months ago we came across a unique item from that collection that we think you may have an interest in. The item is an original typewritten manuscript by Florence Scovel Shinn, *The Magic Path of Intuition.*

We're contacting you to see if you or Hay House have an interest in purchasing this rare original manuscript as we feel you are uniquely positioned to share its content with the world.

Life works in the most wondrous ways. I am continuously astounded as my good comes to me. That this work would be found and come into my hands, just amazed me.

I am thrilled to be publishing this book through Hay House, and I hope you enjoy this beautiful little treasure.

Louise Hay

✛ ✛

THE
MAGIC
PATH OF
INTUITION
(original, unedited text)

THE MAGIC FAITH OF INTUITION

"Prayer is telephoning to God, and intuition is God telephoning to you."

True prayer means preparation. Having made your demands on the Universal Supply for any good thing, act immediately, as if you expected to receive it. Show active faith, thereby impressing the subconscious mind with expectancy.

3

There was a lady who knew the law of preparation and purchased expensive magazines to give herself the feeling of opulence. Intuition told her to buy the magazines. One way to cultivate intuition is to say before sleeping: "In the morning, I'll know just what to do." Ideas will flash before you begin to reason.

Prayer is telephoning to God, and intuition is God telephoning to you. Intuition comes from your superconscious mind. It is God within. The subconscious is simply power without direction. What you feel deeply or say with feeling is impressed upon the subconscious and carried out in the minutest detail. It is your soul and must be restored. Impress the subconscious with the perfect ideas of the superconscious mind instead of the doubts and fears of the conscious mind. Do this by repeating an affirmation: *Stand still and see the power within me.*

Through following intuition, you often go for one thing and get another. From the super-conscious—the realm of intuition—what you should know will be revealed to you. Become very quiet and make affirmations.

You have no need for resentment, resistance, fear, worry, all forms of fighting, etc. The situation you resent will be wiped out. Stand still. Keep your poise, and the Power within will fight your battle. Anger and resentment blur vision and often affect eyesight, as well as prevent you from following your intuitive leads.

For example, you met a friend on the street and you said gaily, "Aren't we having wonderful weather?" She replied, "Yes, but you are looking rather tired." Then you answered, with feeling (making your first false move): "Oh, no! I've never felt more rested in

my life!" Then she replied, "Well, perhaps you look badly because you have such an unbecoming hat."

Filled with resentment, you hurried home to look into the mirror to see what was wrong with the hat. You had a pain in the back of your neck, for your attitude of mind has caused congestion there. From this comes the slang expression: "You give me a pain in the neck." You are now ready to contract a cold or something worse. Call on the law of forgiveness at once. Send love and goodwill to your friend, and say, "Oh, Power Above, give me another chance . . . this time I won't argue. I'll be nonresistant, loving, and kind." Now you have neutralized the congestion and the ensuing ills. The next time you meet your friend, you are filled with goodwill, and you really do not care whether she likes your hat or not. You say, "What a lovely day!" And she will reply,

"How well you look! Where did you get that cute hat?"

There is no emotional response to a situation. You have finished with it; otherwise, you have the same experience over and over again. Poise is the pearl of great price.

✛

The Game of Life is a game of boomerangs. Whatever you send out comes back. Jesus said to do unto others as you would be done by them. You cannot hurt anyone without hurting yourself. All of us are linked by a mysterious magnetic force; what you send out in word or thought against another reacts on yourself. If a person is purely on the mental plane, his comeback (or karma) takes longer. If you are developed spiritually, it returns very quickly; the more you know, the more you are responsible for. So learn your lessons and be thorough with the long road of experience.

Send goodwill to your seeming enemy, and you surround yourself with a great aura of protection. Your enemies are only those of your "own household" (your subconscious beliefs). If you hate and resent a situation, you have fastened it to yourself, for you attract what you fear or dislike. When someone has been unjust to you, you are filled with wrath and resentment. You cannot forgive that person. Time rolls by, and another person does the same thing. It is because you have a picture of injustice engraved in your subconscious. History will repeat itself until you think you are cursed with misfortune and injustice. There is only one way to neutralize it. Be absolutely undisturbed by the injustice, and send goodwill to all concerned. Affirm: *My goodwill is a strong Tower around me. I now change all enemies into friends. All inharmony into harmony. All injustice into justice.*

You will be amazed by the working of the law. One of my students brought harmony out of chaos in her business affairs by using the above statement.

As the alchemists of old transmuted all base metals into gold, you have the power to change all evil into good.

"Therefore I tell you, whatever you ask for in prayer, believe that you have received it, and it will be yours."

— MARK 11:24

✝ ✝

HOW TO WIND YOURSELF UP FINANCIALLY

"Gratitude is the law of increase, and complaint is the law of decrease."

The *material* attitude toward money is to trust in your salary, your income, and your investments, which can shrink overnight. The *spiritual* attitude is to trust in God for your supply—to keep your possessions, and always realize they are God-in-manifestation. If one door closes, immediately, another door opens.

Money is a symbol of freedom and is part of the Divine Plan. There is an invisible supply for you to draw upon. It is the bank of the imagination. In demonstrating prosperity (or other blessings), first speak your word. Affirm this statement: *God is my supply; and big, happy financial surprises now come to me.*

Do something to show your faith. Faith without works is dead. Buy a new bag or wallet, saying, "This is my magic purse to hold the money the Universe sends me." It gives you a feeling of prosperity and expectancy. Now get a new fountain pen and say, "This is a magic pen for endorsing." Give away old clothes that make you feel poor. They will drag you down. This is true prayer, which means preparation. You now feel that you have already received (on the invisible plane). Manifestation will come under grace.

Things should never possess you; you should possess things. Don't have a fear of loss, or your possessions will disappear. You never really possess that which you are in fear of losing, and if you do not appreciate a blessing, it is not impressed upon the subconscious and will fade out of your life.

For example, a lady owned some beautiful pearls. She had great wealth but always talked lack and said repeatedly, "Someday I'll have to eat those pearls." Now her fortune has vanished, and the pearls were sold for food and other necessities.

Words and thoughts are a form of radio-activity, and do not return void. By your words you are justified, and by your words you are condemned. Count your blessings. It is the law of increase. Be grateful for what you have, and you will attract more to be grateful for. Gratitude is the law of increase, and complaint is the law of decrease. Continually give thanks for what you have, and for manifestation of invisible supply.

The following affirmation has brought wonderful results: *I give thanks that the Universe is my supply; and I am now linked with endless streams of steady, ready money, under grace in perfect ways.* Another good statement is: *I shall not want, for my supply precedes me. Faith must become a habit.*

No matter how much money you have, if you feel poor, you begin to lose money. Nothing comes into your life uninvited. You are always inviting poverty or prosperity through your quality of thought. Now is the appointed time. *Today is the day of my amazing good*

fortune. All day affirm silently a statement of truth to counteract negative thoughts: *As money goes out, I touch a hidden spring, which releases large sums of money to return to me, under grace, in miraculous ways.*

It does not mean that you throw money away or spend foolishly. It means that you are fearless in following your intuitive leads to spend or to give.

For example, a woman had an intuitive lead to give a friend who had been very helpful to her a hundred dollars. Soon after that she received a *thousand* dollars from an unexpected source.

Do not be afraid to make large demands on the Bank of Faith and Trust, Company of the Universe, but you cannot attract more than you feel at home with. If you feel at home with millions, millions will feel at home with you. Financial freedom is God's idea for man. "What God has done before, he can do for me and more" opens doors. Do not look back and hash over hard times, or you'll be drawn back into these conditions. Give thanks for the dawn of a new day. You must be immune to all discouragement and adverse appearances. Affirm: *The tide has turned to stay, for the Universe has right of way.*

"So shall thy barns be filled with plenty."

— PROVERBS 3:10

✛ ✛

19

THE MAGIC PATH OF INTUITION

"What you see with your inner eye you meet sooner or later on the external."

Awaken, you that sleep. All that you desire or require is already on your pathway, but you must be wide-awake to your good to bring it into manifestation. Affirm: *The Power within <u>sweeps</u> out of my mind, body, and affairs everything not divinely planned, and puts my house in order, now and forevermore!*

The word *sweeps* gives you a picture of action. This spiritual broom sweeps out all belief in lack, loss, failure, resentment, inharmony, sadness, etc. You are asleep to your good while these negative thoughts clutter your mental house. You resent someone, thereby giving that person power to harm you. You feel you are a failure, therefore missing your opportunity for brilliant success. You are overwhelmed with a feeling of loss, and that friends and prosperity have gone from your life. You are still asleep in the "dream of opposites." Wake up and you will find a new world of health, wealth, and happiness, with every desire of your heart fulfilled.

It is brought about by your *word*, for your word is your wand. When in the deepest despair is the time to wave your word over the situation. Baptize every failure by saying "Success!" Never let the third dimension interfere

with the fourth dimension. The third dimension is the world of adverse appearances; it is the fog most people live in. Your affirmation dissipates the fog, and the sun is out. Affirm: *The sun now comes out in my mind and body, and I see clearly the fulfillment of my heart's desire.*

Your dreary desires are answered drearily. Your impatient desires are long delayed or violently fulfilled. You long for flowers and say, "Poor me! No one ever sends me any." One day you walk along the street and a pot of geraniums hits you on the head. These are your flowers, but not under grace in a perfect way. You should have said, "I give thanks that my flowers come from the Universe, under grace in a perfect way." Then they would have been received through the right channels.

This is the law of nature: Use or lose. Hoarding and saving always lead to loss. Use what you have, and more will be added unto you. If you save for a rainy day, or in case of sickness, they are sure to come. Use money you have freely, but with wisdom, knowing your invisible supply is always at hand. Soon the law of accumulation will be set in action; abundance will pour in and pile up.

Never say, "I am broke," as it impresses the subconscious with a picture of emptiness. The Game of Life is a game of *Solitaire*. As you change, so do your affairs. Affirm: *I am now immune to all hurts and frustrations. The Power within is perfect peace and perfect poise.*

A student once told me her mother always "made scenes" on holidays. At her sister's home, the mother said, "I never want to dine in this house again." Next year, she was in the hospital. The student visited, and the mother said, "God has sent me this trial, so I will bear it patiently." The student replied, "Mother, God didn't send you this illness; *you* attracted it yourself by your angry words. You said you didn't want to dine at Hannah's again, and here you are." The mother replied, "Oh, let me alone. I prefer my old God who sends trials and tribulations." The student asked her to think constructively while in the hospital—to see herself walking into Hannah's house, well and happy. The mother did so and was well again within a few weeks, to the surprise of the doctors.

✣

What you see with your inner eye (the imaging faculty) you meet sooner or later on the external. So see clearly your goodness, your health, your success, your happiness; and they will come to pass. Faith brings fruit.

I am often asked why it is easier to see failure than success, unhappiness than happiness. It is of our early training, which was usually negative. When good things happened, people exclaimed, "This is too good to be true." Millions of people have neutralized their good by this attitude, for you are accountable for your "idle words." They impress the subconscious and are carefully carried out. Affirm: *I see vividly my immediate and endless supply. It comes from a Higher Power, and all doors fly open! All channels are free. I see vividly my radiant health, perfect and permanent. I see vividly my heart's desires come to pass in the twinkling of an eye.*

Do not visualize or force a picture. It will flash into your consciousness from the superconscious. A powerful statement is: *The light of lights streams through my mind, body, and affairs, revealing all in Divine order. I see clearly there are*

*no obstacles on my pathway. I see clearly the open
road of fulfillment.*

It is important also to have happy sur-
roundings. No dreary pictures. Keep your desk
in order. Have fresh blotting paper handy.
There is nothing like fresh blotting paper for
attracting big checks. An orderly consciousness is a rich consciousness.

A London newspaper told a story of African
chiefs who toured the city. Nothing impressed
them until they saw the subway and an esca-
lator. They were immediately entranced and
exclaimed, "Ah! The ground walks." Affirm: *I
am now on the ground that walks, which takes me
right to my promised land, in a magical way.*

Don't sing sad songs. Your subconscious is
impressed by anything you feel deeply. Your
word is your wand. Nothing is too good to be

true. Nothing is too wonderful to happen or too good to last.

"Order is heaven's first law."

— ALEXANDER POPE

✢ ✢

How to Break Up Old Thought-Forms

*"No one keeps you out
of your good but yourself."*

A negative idea, continually dwelled upon, will create a thought-form in the subconscious. These thought-forms will meet you on your pathway of life until you neutralize them. If you are filled with suspicion, you soon find what you are looking for. What you fear, you attract, and nothing can save you but neutralizing your fears. Act fearless and walk up to the lions in your way. Your fears will externalize in concrete experiences.

Affirm: *I give thanks for my whirlwind success. I sweep all before me, for I work with the Spirit and follow the Divine Plan of my life. The decks are cleared for Divine action.* This affirmation is very strong, for it brings a feeling of tremendous power. Old thought-forms dissolve, and the Divine idea of success takes its place.

Don't call someone a "poor Nellie." You help demagnetize her. The human mind is helpless to cope with these negative thoughts. The victory is won by the God within the superconscious mind. Affirm: *I am magnetized by the Universe. I have and hold, from this day forth, and forevermore, all that is mine by Divine right.*

In the story of Cinderella, her stepmother and stepsisters were the thought-forms she had built up in her consciousness. Nearly everyone has a cruel stepmother in their subconscious—keeping them out of their good—usually called an inferiority complex. The Fairy Godmother appears to tell her that she *can* go to the ball and have the things she desires. The Fairy Godmother is the superconscious mind, the God within, with whom all things are possible. Cinderella loses her glass slipper and gets her desire, her Prince.

Your fears make a galley slave of you, so call on the Power within to set you free. Affirm: *All things are possible here and now. I now attain the seemingly unattainable.*

Taking a trip often breaks up old thought-forms, for it brings a change of scene and environment—new thoughts. People travel

many miles to take a "cure" of some kind and return as a "different person." People who come to Vichy and Carlsbad are greatly benefited because they left their worries behind. Natives keep fears and receive no benefits.

Don't build up an envy thought-form; it keeps you out of the promised land (yours). You build yourself a prison. No one keeps you out of your good but yourself. A thought-form of self-pity is one of the most dangerous you can have. The more you pity yourself, the worse things get.

Be above the worry belt, in consciousness, and then you will have instantaneous manifestations. Your success, happiness, or abundance comes to pass in the "twinkling of an eye."

"Let not your heart be troubled, neither be afraid."

— JOHN 14:27

✝ ✝

HEALTH AND HAPPINESS

"A harmonious person is never vibrating at the same rate as a germ."

Health and happiness go hand in hand. Ill health is caused by inharmony. A teacher says he never asks a student, "What is the matter with you?" I ask, "Who is the matter with you?" As long as anyone can cause you to be angry, resentful, irritable, sad, etc., a harmful reaction takes place in the cells of your body, producing some sort of disease.

For example, a woman was wrongly deprived of $200. I told her to bless the person responsible, be undisturbed, and draw the $200 from the Universal Supply, for if one door shuts, another door opens. She said she couldn't, and from these negative thoughts came a trial of ills. She wondered why had she attracted the situation. I replied, "But you have always held an iron grip on money. You counted every penny, and saved and economized when you had the intuitive lead to spend or give. Saving is a good idea, but it can't be done, for you are violating the law of use. Then comes karmic reactions, and you have a landslide of loss, wiping out the money you should have kept in circulation. Often a landslide of loss comes through violating intuition."

Lack and loss affect the health, such as with financial headaches. Continual criticism

and faultfinding produce acid deposits in the
blood, which causes rheumatism. Hate and
resentment generate a poison in the system
that produces disease. A chemical change
is produced in a person's body by suddenly
changing from despair to joy. Fear and despair produce congestion and disease, while
joy releases the proper circulation and health
is regained.

*Now is the appointed time. Today is the day
of amazing prosperity.* This affirmation would
bring an immediate change in world affairs.
Life and death are in the power of the tongue,
as is success or failure and lack or abundance,
for words and thoughts are a form of radio-
activity. Man must learn to draw from the
Universal Supply for everything. This will do
away with all poverty and limitation, which
are states of mind.

We live in a great sea of magnetic force called mind-stuff, which continually takes the form of man's desires. The body can be remolded by treatment, which is clear vision and an affirmation. I once told a patient to see herself bathed in the dazzling white light of the Spirit, which dissolves everything not divinely planned. See yourself bathed in the dazzling Light of Lights daily, and age will not register in the cells of your body. "Don't be dejected and sad, for the joy of the Lord is your strength." Joy brings new strength, vigor, and vitality. Worry and fear tear down the cells of the body.

Many healthy people have become nervous wrecks from losing money—their hair turning prematurely gray within a short time. People who have knowledge of spiritual Truth come through big financial losses, looking and

feeling as if always on the crest of the wave. Being undisturbed by the appearance of loss, the money was restored.

For example, a woman came to me who had lost $30,000 when an investor used the money for himself. The lawyer told her she would never recover it. I told her to bless the man and forgive him, but claim the $30,000 from the Abundance of Spheres. If one door shuts, another would open. I added, "Never feel sorry for yourself, and do everything you can to keep feeling rich." She did. Friends who met her on the street said, "We don't have to ask you how you are. You look like a million dollars."

In a few months the miracle happened: the money was refunded. She had kept herself vibrating to success and prosperity; it could not help coming to her.

A person who is low-spirited or inharmonious will contract a cold; a happy, fearless person will be immune to germs. For example, a woman goes out in cold weather in evening clothes—lightly clad—but is quite comfortable, for she feels she is looking well and is filled with anticipation for a happy evening. If the same woman is dressed in an unbecoming gown or in a bad humor, she will come back complaining of a cold and discomfort and have a cough the next day. A harmonious person is never vibrating at the same rate as a germ.

Fear and resentment affect eyesight, and stubbornness and strong personal will affect hearing. If you are feeling bored, discouraged, or listless, do something to wind yourself up, which means changing your vibration, and repeat an affirmation continually: *A wonderful joy is on its way, and this wonderful joy comes to stay.*

A person with a torpid liver is always blue and depressed. He thinks it is the liver that gives him this negative attitude of mind, but it is quite the reverse, for *he* is the matter with his liver. What affects the liver is condemnation —too much discrimination, faultfinding, caution, sorrow, vain regrets, and jealousy. You ask, "Why shouldn't a person be discriminating and cautious?" If ruled by discrimination and caution, you are not listening to your intuitive lead, which often sends you in a direction your reasoning mind rebels against. The liver is a very sensitive organ and is quickly affected by wrong thinking. The ancients, for that reason, name it the *liver*, meaning "the place you live."

Anger, fear, cruel thoughts, etc., affect the heart. A good statement to use is the following: *The Light of Lights streams through my mind, body, and affairs, revealing all in Divine order. My heart is a happy heart, a fearless heart,*

THE MAGIC PATH OF INTUITION

a forgiving heart, a kind heart, in its right place, doing its right work.

Skin diseases are caused by mental irritation. Someone has gotten "under your skin." Often instantaneous healings take place in this way, by a sudden realization of the Truth. Your body, in reality, is a spiritual body, incorruptible and indestructible, "timeless and tireless, birthless and deathless." When all negative thinking is wiped out, you will be enveloped by your Light Body, and sorrow and sighing will have passed away and death itself overcome.

"Don't be dejected and sad, for the joy of the Lord is your strength."

— NEHEMIAH 8:10

✝ ✝

BRINGING YOUR FUTURE INTO THE NOW

"You must live fully in the now to make your dreams come true."

Time and space are but a dream. Man must bring his future into the now. Blessings that seem so far away in the future are already prepared for you, waiting for you to believe in manifestation.

For example, a student desired a watch. I told her to believe she already received it, and she soon received it from a friend.

Realization is manifestation. You ask how can you get rid of doubts and fears, which prevent realization? The answer is by taking an affirmation that gives a feeling of security and satisfaction. If you are afraid of a big dog, say, "Beat it, you big bluff." The courts, fears, and adverse appearances are certainly only big bluffs.

A man who worried continually, seeming impossible to stop his worrisome thoughts, took out his watch and said he would worry for half an hour. To his surprise he found it impossible to worry, for he had put the law of nonresistance into operation. We ask the Universal Supply and then sigh, "I'll not get it." The successful man walks to hidden music.

With rhythm in his thoughts, all the traffic goes his way. He has lucky breaks. Out of luck, out of rhythm. Affirm: *The tide has turned to stay, for God has right of way.*

You turned the tide; it brings joy and abundance. *You* gave the right of way. This brings your future into the now. Show active faith to turn the tide.

Some people always live in the future. It is daydreaming, and they never catch up with the now. One brother had a big vision and went to a large city where he linked up with opportunities that brought him fame and fortune. The other boy spent time telling people what he would do when he got a million dollars. He never got further than his rural audience. You must live fully in the now to make your dreams come true, but always be sure that you are dreaming according to the

Divine Plan. There is a Divine Design of your life in your subconscious mind, so unless the Divine dreams the dream, they labor in vain who dream it. Affirm: *Let the Divine Design of my life flash into my conscious mind. Let me see clearly the perfect plan.*

The conscious mind must be redeemed from its wrong thinking by giving it the right ideas to work from the superconscious. You may desire something that is not in the Divine Plan, and you find you are continually blocked in its manifestation; or if you attain it, it brings only unhappiness and misfortune. Health, wealth, love, and perfect self-expression are the square of life and are for each individual, but the way of manifestation belongs to the Great Designer.

For example, the store sends two sweaters instead of the particular one the customer ordered. She picked one she had not at first selected and liked this one much better. After that she gladly left the selection of everything in life to Infinite Intelligence. *The Universal Power is in my ship. I now sail fearlessly in unknown seas.*

Many people are afraid of new undertakings. They are panic-stricken by the idea of doing something different, even though old conditions are unbearable. Sail joyously in unknown seas; arrive in your promised land. People wear out doing the same things every day. Have some interesting recreation to use a new set of brain cells. In order to be successful, the element of play must enter into what you are doing.

Let the ideal be the only reality in your life—then the obstacles and hindrances will melt away, as you are undisturbed by them.

The Spirit is Pure Intelligence, upon which man draws to tune in. Do not limit yourself to a one-station radio of life. Tune in with Infinite Intelligence. Look with amazement at that which is before you.

With the fixed idea that your supply comes from Infinite Intelligence, you will always be provided for, in both big and little ways. The big things in life will come easily if you have no doubts or fears. So live fully in today, and bring your future into the now.

"Behold, I say unto you, lift up your eyes and look on the fields; for they are white already to harvest."

— JOHN 4:35

✛ ✛

THE HOUSE THAT FAITH BUILT

"Faith is simply knowing that God can do it."

Hebrews 11:1 says: "Now faith is the substance of things hoped for, the evidence of things not seen." This is a scientific statement, for as we live in a sea of magnetic force, called mind-stuff, what we imagine is impressed upon this sensitive substance and crystallizes, sooner or later, on the external. The experiences you meet in life are your own creations. Henry Wadsworth Longfellow said, "A man's life is the history of his fears." Why not make it the history of your faith so someday you can say, "This is the health that faith built! This is the wealth that faith built! This is the success and happiness that faith built!"

Doubts and fears are sins, for they impress negative pictures on the mind-stuff and bring lack, limitation, or disaster to pass. Have faith in the affirmations you use. Never use a statement that does not give you a feeling of security.

Faith is like the Gulf Stream, a river flowing through the ocean. Faith brings warmth and will change conditions for you.

For example, a woman came to me with the appearance of a flesh growth. It was quite noticeable and long-standing, but she had perfect faith that it could be healed. Weeks passed by without any apparent change, but she said, "I have perfect faith that God is doing His perfect work." One day, it suddenly disappeared! Her friends were amazed and said, "You had better go to a doctor and see what happened." She replied, "I am perfectly well. God has done His perfect work."

Faith is simply knowing that God can do it. Every unpleasant condition in your life is the result of a lack of faith. A student demonstrated several thousand dollars after years of lack, but her first act was prompted by fear instead of faith. "I bought a lot of shoes in case I should be without money again." Her motive was wrong. Watch your own motives with all diligence, for out of them are the issues of life. If her motive had been simply a desire for plenty of shoes, it would have been constructive. But it was really a preparation for loss, so she soon had lots of shoes but no money.

Many people keep back their demonstrations by fretting because of evildoers. Someone is mean; someone is unjust or cruel. Resentment is a violation of the law of love (goodwill) and is a barrier to your desires. "Trust in the Lord and do good" means to never doubt the power of God. Trust Infinite Intelligence with the management of your affairs, never interfere with doubts or worry, and let every act be prompted by good motives.

✝

Follow your intuitive leads and prepare for the blessings you have asked for, regardless of adverse appearances. True prayer means preparation. For example, a lady wanted a radio, made a place for it in the corner, and kept the spot dusted. If your demonstration lags, you haven't dusted it. The explorer and adventurer in you will see you through. It is your Divine Self, the superconscious, which knows no defeat or failure. With fearless faith, mountains

are removed from your subconscious; therefore, they disappear in the external.

The lions on your pathway will be powerless to harm you when you turn to the Universal Power for protection and send goodwill to the lions. You can never receive what you cannot see yourself receiving, for everything comes through you, not to you. An athlete said he was working on his broad jump; he was lying there, seeing a win. A person with a success consciousness is someone who doesn't know he is a failure, even when he fails. His vision of success is strong—he is unmoved by adverse conditions.

Keep yourself wound up. Activate faith. Affirm: *I am wide-awake to my good. I never miss a trick.*

We have often heard people say that certain things are bad for our health, but we have never heard them say that certain things are bad for wealth. Broken chairs, untidiness, disorder, etc., are bad for wealth, for they keep us in a poor vibration. A man told me he had put his life in order by straightening out his desk. He threw out old letters, pieces of twine, and faded ink-filled blotters, and pigeonholed the papers he wanted and were important. Conditions on the external changed. A new world of order and prosperity opened for him.

As you change in consciousness, all the conditions about you change. Do not neglect the day of small things, for little beginnings have big endings.

"According to your faith be it done unto you."

— MATTHEW 9:29

✦ ✦

Do Not Let
Your Heart's
Desire Become a
Heart's Disease

*"Every test is a process
of purification."*

Many people do not receive their heart's desire because they desire it too intensely. They are longing for it instead of feeling they have already received it. If you believed that before you called, you were answered, then you would be quite free from worry and anxiety, and live joyfully in the moment. When you can be happy with or without your heart's desire, it will suddenly appear, for your ship will come in over a "don't care" sea. Be happy, and something will happen. Feel rich, and riches will manifest on the external.

All suffering is a spiritual alarm clock. You have been asleep about something. Perhaps you have been unjust, unforgiving, ungrateful, critical, or intolerant. Perhaps you were afraid to follow an intuitive lead. Suddenly the karmic factories begin working, for the "way of the transgressor is hard."

For example, you have condemned someone, and now someone condemns you. You were unjust; someone is now unjust to you. You were intolerant; someone is intolerant toward you, etc. You are now awake, and instead of blaming people or circumstances for your unhappiness, you look back to see why you attracted the situation. Someone you disliked harmed you, but you gave that person power to hurt you, because you withheld love and goodwill. Your own poisoned arrows have returned to you. Now call on the law of forgiveness and affirm the statement: *I call on the law of forgiveness. I am free from mistakes. I am under grace and not under karmic law.* Forgive the person or persons who have harmed you, sending love and goodwill, saying, "I forgive them." Then like a kaleidoscope, the whole situation changes, for love is the fulfilling of the law. Your seeming enemies are transmuted into friends and, consciously or unconsciously, serve the Divine Plan of your life.

One learns tolerance through suffering. If your unhappy experiences make you bitter and resentful, you will attract more of the

Hate

Hate

Hate

LOVE

Hate

Hate

same variety. Make the most of your karma so that the experiences will not be repeated. The fear of the law is the beginning of wisdom.

I was in the toy department of a crowded shop one day, and a little boy was standing in front of a huge bear, which moved its head up and down and looked quite ferocious. A stranger leaned over and asked, "Little boy, aren't you afraid of that big bear?" He replied, "No, ma'am, bears don't bite good little boys." He had a clear conscience and was unafraid.

To receive the desire of the heart, all karma must be wiped out, as well as anxiety, impatience, and fear. We are told to wait patiently on the law. Patience means nonresistance. Practice nonresistance on the law, and it will bring your desire to pass.

I heard a man say, "The good Lord takes his time. He's the one man you can't hurry."

It came to me as a direct message, for I had become impatient and was trying to force a demonstration. I suddenly realized that the more patient (nonresistant) I was, the quicker the Universe could work. Soon the demonstration came in, over a calm sea. People so often keep back a demonstration of their good by outlining the channels. Happy is the man who believes that Infinite Intelligence knows the way of fulfillment.

For example, a woman had a business enterprise she wished to develop. She tried every avenue she could think of, but no one was interested enough to help her. She became nonresistant and put it in the Universe's hands, saying, "I'll let the Universe attend to this. I let go." She was visiting in a distant city and met a woman, seemingly quite by chance, who asked her if she might carry out the enterprise. The Universe is eternal, reliable, and unchangeable but must be given the "right of way."

Personal will keeps you out of your own kingdom. For example, a friend came to me saying she would be obliged to sell a piece of jewelry in order to have ready cash. She did not want to sell it and regretted that it was necessary to do so. I said, "Why, this pin isn't your pin—it is the Divine Spirit's pin. We now place it upon the altar. If it is Spirit's will, you will sell it; if not, you will receive the money in some other way." A few days later she telephoned and said, "I didn't have to sell the pin! I received an unexpected check that supplied the money I needed." She had applied this wonderful law of renunciation, which is so difficult for many people to understand.

✢

The desire of the heart can only be attained through nonresistance. For example, one of my students said that the man she cared for was very cruel and indifferent. She was looking forward to spending New Year's Eve with him, when he suddenly announced that he had another engagement for the night. She was shedding tears of anger and resentment. I said, "You are completely demagnetized; therefore, you are pushing your good away from you. When you see him, don't be angry and reproachful. Bless him and say that you wish him a happy evening." She did this, much to his surprise. He couldn't understand her change in attitude. The following day he called her on the telephone and asked if he might spend New Year's Eve with her. There was nothing more said about his former plans.

At one of my meetings at the Unity Society, I gave the following treatment to dissolve

all anger and resentment: *The light of Infinite Intelligence streams through your consciousness, dissolving and dissipating all anger and resentment. You are at peace with yourself and with the whole world.* A woman told me, after the meeting, that she seems enveloped in a blazing light, which swept all discord from her consciousness, forever. She said, "When you were speaking, I realized I had lost everything I ever loved through anger, but now I feel that I can never be angry again. It was a most wonderful experience."

Many people think if they can control their temper or not show anger, it is enough. This is not the case. The vibration goes out just the same. As long as you can be moved inwardly, there will be discord in your life. You must be cleansed to be free from anger and the effects of anger. Don't let appearances rock your boat. I had a patient who once said,

"I should have been mad, but I wasn't. I should have been afraid, but I wasn't." This showed spiritual growth.

In your subconscious are the negative tidbits and beliefs impressed upon it from your many life experiences. Thus, it must be renewed by flooding it with the perfect ideas of the superconscious, your Divine Self. Love and goodwill to all is the goal. I knew a man who said, "Of course I love everybody, but there are a lot of people I don't like." I replied, "No, you still have some spots of ill will in your consciousness; you will have to be sent back to the cleaners." Every test is a process of purification. When we are unmoved by them, we won't attract them.

I have a friend who says that whenever she needs money, she takes a taxicab to make herself feel rich. One stormy and slushy day, she

had a definite lead to take a taxi. She told me, "I argued with my rich heavenly Father and said, 'God, I would rather save the dollar and take the subway.' So, I had my way and took the subway, but when I reached home, I found that I had lost a dollar." The most expensive thing you can do is to violate a hunch. If money is not used for the right purposes, it will go in some uninteresting or unhappy way.

The minute you make your demand, Infinite Spirit knows the way of fulfillment. Only doubt, fear, or reasoning keeps away your good. Live fully in the wonderful now, with joyful expectance, knowing that God is the How, God is the When, and God is the Where.

You must answer each negative thought with a word of authority. If you entertain them or give them attention, "the army of aliens" will encamp in your consciousness.

Your doubts and fears and resentments will settle down to stay, bringing a harvest of misfortune. A good affirmation is: *As I am one with the All-Powerful Spirit, I am one with my good, for Spirit is my good in immediate action.* Your blessing is already there, waiting for you to believe it is possible to accomplish. Worry and fear will push it away from you.

Sometimes a demonstration comes to pass through a counterirritant. A student told me she had wanted a certain business enterprise to be a success. She agonized and fretted over it. Then something else came into her life to worry her, which took her thoughts completely off the business. She forgot to worry about it. Suddenly she had a telephone message saying the deal had gone over, followed by a large check. She had shifted her worry thoughts long enough for the deal to go through.

When you have completely put to flight your worries, there will be nothing to interfere with the immediate manifestation of every good and perfect gift, for your heart's desire is no longer a heart's disease.

"The Lord is my shepherd,
I shall not want."

— PSALM 23

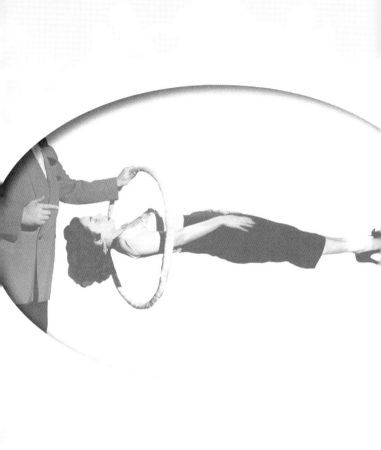

INFINITE
INTELLIGENCE,
THE GREAT MAGICIAN

*"When you realize that time and
space are but a dream, you live
suspended in the moment, and
time can never touch you."*

Magic and *miracle* come from the same root
word. It is a good thing to go see a magician
once in a while, to get the realization of things
coming suddenly from apparently nowhere.
Of course with the magician, it is a trick. Out

of his hat come rabbits and ducks; out of his sleeve, a bowl of goldfish.

Now we must get the realization that with Infinite Intelligence, the seemingly impossible can come to pass. The Universal Power, the Great Magician, changes a curse into a blessing, despair into joy, lack into plenty, sickness into health, etc. There is no limit to the good that God has prepared for man. Only doubt or unbelief shuts off the Power within each man.

However, faith turns the Power on again, so it is necessary to do everything to develop faith in that Power. Sometimes a new affirmation or a new idea will suddenly give you the realization, which is manifestation.

In one of my classes, I explained that it was necessary to "become as a little child" in order to be a good demonstrator and bring in the element of play. Then I said, "Let us look upon the Universal Power as the Great Magician and draw out of His hat whatever we desire or require." This eliminates all questioning as to the channel. We see simply the Giver of the Gift. One man present was in the real-estate business, and a few days afterward, he was asked by his firm to locate a seven-story building in a certain district for a client. It seemed impossible to find just what he wanted, and he became discouraged. Then he thought of the Great Magician's hat. He closed his eyes and said, "I now draw from the Great Magician's hat, the right seven-story building in the right location." Very soon after that, he walked into the building that was suitable in every way.

Be wide-awake to your good, and let every event of the day teach you something. For example, I had taken my watch to the jeweler's to be repaired, and after waiting a month it

was returned, but lost ten minutes a day. I felt a little annoyed. When putting it on my wrist, it fell out of my hand onto the hardwood floor. I was meek and nonresistant by this time, and exclaimed, "I baptize it 'Success'!" (See the chapter called "The Law of Nonresistance" in *The Game of Life and How to Play It*.) I picked it up and it was still ticking, so I put it on and went out. The following day it was ticking away quite normally and, much to my surprise, kept perfect time. In falling it had become regulated. So if you have a bump of any kind, know you are being regulated, and you'll come out of it much improved. The person who resists and resents will have to be regulated many times.

Your supply is always with you, as it is prepared long beforehand. The following is a good statement: *Reveal to me the Great Magician's Storehouse. I now use the field glasses of the spirit.* Make believe you have the spiritual field glasses, which bring faraway blessings very near. With these field glasses, you see avalanches of checks, bills, and currency. You see health, happiness, success, etc. Do not visualize. Let the Divine ideas flash into your conscious mind. You are now linking with your invisible supply, which manifests on the external, through the consciousness of having received. Worry, doubt, and fear blur your spiritual field glasses. They must be continually cleaned with fresh inspiration and faith. Maybe a friend's faith in you will give you faith in yourself.

There is always some way of being recharged, like a battery, and suddenly the Divine Plan will unfold right at your feet, for the ground you are on is harvest ground.

All unhappiness comes from not being able to see clearly your good. So, if assailed by doubts and fears, do something immediately to show your faith.

A woman came to me to speak the word for her perfect home. She was living in a small room in a hotel. She was discouraged, so I told her to "dig a ditch" (see the chapter called "The Law of Prosperity" in *The Game of Life and How to Play It*) to do something to show faith. She returned one day with a long package. She said to me, "Bless it." I asked, "What is it?" She replied, "A carving knife. It's something I have no use for in a hotel." So her active faith, which is preparation, opened the way for her divinely designed home.

✢

Life is an arena where you prove Infinite Intelligence as your defense and your deliverance, and your immediate and endless supply of all good. If you say you are going to do a thing and then do not attend to it, it will be done for you violently when you least expect it. For example, I had a ribbon belt on a dress with long streamers that ended in tassels. One streamer, I thought, was too long, and I said repeatedly, "I must shorten that tassel." I never got around to it, as they say in the country, and one day I was climbing to the top seat of a bus, when I felt a jerk and a rip. I looked down and the tassel had been torn off, making it just the length I had intended to have it. This was an unimportant experience, but it taught me not to say I was going to do a thing and then not do it. Despise not the day of small things.

A woman told me the following story, proving the reality of her invisible supply: It was in the early spring. She wanted some

apple blossoms and started out in her car to go to the nearest farmer. She went to one after another, being told by each farmer that it was too early in the season for apple blossoms. Undiscouraged, she made a final attempt. She drove up to the next farmhouse to ask and had the same reply. She looked over at the orchard and exclaimed, "Why, there are blossoms on one of those trees." The farmer replied, "Those blossoms came out after your arrival here." Trust in God, and the seemingly impossible will come to pass.

I knew a man who at 60 was bankrupt, and at 76 was making $30,000 a year. He said his success came after he stopped worrying, which was after he was bankrupt. His new ships of success came in over an unworried sea.

Time will register in your body and affairs so long as you believe in it. When you realize that time and space are but a dream, you live suspended in the moment, and time can never touch you.

This is the consciousness of those who have become "ascended masters." Jesus Christ said, "In the world [of three dimensions] ye shall have tribulation, but be of good cheer for I have overcome the world." He had overcome the thought-world of lack, limitation, and death itself and made the ascension. Jesus blessed the loaves and fishes, and immediately came the increase. It was because he had the unshakable conviction that the Infinite Intelligence within accomplished the work. He taught this to his disciples and the people. He did not claim anymore for himself than he did for others. After 2,000 years, we realize the amazing simplicity of his teachings.

I have often said that most people look too closely for their demonstrations, trying to force a channel or speculate upon the results of every move. There are three simple rules for taking every trick in the Game of Life: *speak* the word, *follow* your hunches, and *dig* your ditches. You will then be kept busy living with the wonderful *now* and won't limit the Universe by looking to channels.

In one of my classes we brought up the old proverb, "The watched pot never boils." One of the students said, "We should have a whistling teakettle, which does not have to be watched. When it boils, it whistles for you." So it is with your demonstration, it will whistle for you when it is ready, and when you are ready for it. Many people are asking for conditions that they would not be big enough to handle. You have to grow up to your demonstration. You heart's desire is ripe, but you are green.

I have known women who were filled with doubt, fear, and suspicion ask for perfect love and companionship. It would appear in their lives for a short time, but then be tragically ended, for the old fears and suspicions were stronger than love and faith.

Your good must be built upon the rock of fearless faith. Ideals will be made real if held without wavering. It is useless to say we have faith and then act to the contrary. Action impresses the subconscious, and if you run away from a situation, it will run after you. The only way you can neutralize fear is to walk up to the thing you are afraid of.

Self-pity is one of the deadly sins. "Poor me" is the worst affirmation you can make, as it cuts you off from the Power within, and you will have more and more reasons for pitying yourself. I give the example of a woman who came to me, feeling she was neglected and left out of all the good things in life. I gave her the affirmation: *There is nothing too good for me!* She repeated it hundreds of times, and suddenly, conditions commenced to change. Kind and influential friends came into her life, and new opportunities for success and prosperity opened. Later she was given the desire of her heart, which was to go abroad and study music. Bruce Barton says, "There is danger in being sorry for yourself."

Return to that Infinite Intelligence, the Great Magician, for "I will even make a way in the wilderness and rivers in the desert."

"I will liken him unto a wise man, which built his house upon a rock."

— MATTHEW 7:24

✝ ✝

ALL THAT THE FOURTH DIMENSION AFFORDS IS YOURS

"You will obtain magic results when you really give this Supreme Intelligence the right of way."

The fourth-dimensional world is the world of perfect ideas. As these ideas are established in consciousness, they must come forth on the external, for your world is crystallized thought. Most people have crystallized wrong conditions, for they have served fear instead of faith. It takes a great stretch of the imagination to believe that life can be made perfect, free from all unhappy experiences. Then when you do believe it, it takes a great effort of will to keep on believing when all outward appearances are against you.

"Judge not by appearances." All miracles are founded upon this idea. We can change conditions only by not believing (or being undisturbed) by appearances. I said to a woman who was in great distress, "None of these appearances fools you." It gripped her consciousness, and the Divine Plan of her good won out. We can no longer have the faith of a peasant; we must have an understanding of faith.

Through knowledge of spiritual law, we control conditions. While talking to a student who was confronted by a financial problem, I said, "Stand aside and let God do it." She replied, "That's all there is to it," and soon a new channel opened for her supply. Yes, that *is* all there is to it. Let God do it.

After all your reading and studying of metaphysics and ancient philosophies, etc., you find that they are teaching you just one thing: to let God do it.

Eastern philosophy says, "Let the warrior within you fight." Countless times this idea appears in all sacred writings. North American Indians believe that the Great Spirit is the source of their power. A woman who visited the Indians told me she had interviewed an Indian who had been running all day, carrying a message. She asked him if he did not feel fatigued. He replied, "Me no tired; Big Spirit in me runs." Trusting God must become a habit, and it often takes a long time to form this habit.

I was inspired by reading about Omaha, the famous racehorse, in the paper. The article said, "Omaha has run a mile before he gets into his stride." I said at one of my meetings, "There are a lot of Omahas in this room. You have not yet got into your spiritual stride, but I see you all winning your race in the twinkling of an eye." Often discontent keeps you from getting into your stride. You are dissatisfied with yourself and conditions. You wish you were someone else. How wonderful to be a beautiful movie star, or an heiress of countless millions. On one of my trips to London, I saw advertised the wonderful title of a song. It was called "I'm Tickled to Death I'm Me."

The first start toward success is to be glad you are yourself, and know that the ground you are on is holy ground and that you expand into the Divine Plan of your life. In the Divine Plan, every righteous desire of the

heart is satisfied. You are the leading lady in your life's scenario. You never take a backseat in the fourth dimension. The Divine Plan unfolds through following intuition.

Claude Bragdon says, "To live intuitively is to live fourth dimensionally." The magic path leads you out of the house of bondage and into your promised land. It is the path of destiny, where your failures are transmuted into successes and handicaps prove stepping-stones.

I heard the following story over the radio, which gives a wonderful example. A man who could neither read nor write tried to obtain the position of janitor in a public school. They refused him on account of his illiteracy, so a friend got him a position selling cigars. He became very successful, selling hundreds of cigars, and deposited the money in the bank with the aid of a friend who wrote the deposit slips. After a number of years, he found he had deposited $30,000 and decided to draw some out. The paying teller said, "Write a check for the amount you want to draw out." The man replied, "I can't read or write." The paying teller was amazed and exclaimed, "Good Lord, man. You have accumulated $30,000 without an education! Where would you have been if you had been able to read and write?" The man replied, "I would have been a janitor in Public School No. 1."

In Hyde Park Corner in London, people are permitted to mount soapboxes, collect an audience, and express their views on any subject—religious, political, or personal— saying just what they please regarding the reigning family, etc. The government thinks it is a good way to allow them to let off steam. In passing, I stopped to listen to a poor, forlorn individual who was yelling at the top of his

voice, "There ain't no God, and I can prove it!" I thought, *You have never proved God, or you wouldn't be where you are*. If I had had a copy of *The Game of Life and How to Play it* with me, I would certainly have laid it on his soapbox with a blessing.

We prove God by showing active faith, which puts to flight all adverse appearances. There is nothing left out in the fourth dimension.

✛

I have often been asked, "If the Infinite Intelligence supplies all our needs, why is it necessary to pray for anything?" I answered, "Because that is the law." Man must make the first move. You must press the button in order to turn on the electric light. Many people never make big demands on the Universal Supply. They think it is asking too much. One woman came to me and asked, "Is it wrong to ask for the things that you really want, or should you just ask for necessities?" I replied, "What are the things you really want?" She said, "Love and beauty." I replied, "If you desire them, they are necessities."

When you have the fixed idea that there is only One Power in the Universe, all appearances of evil will disappear from your world. Trouble comes from a belief in duality—good and evil. In getting a demonstration, we must know that the Infinite Intelligence is the only power. Evil comes from "man's vain imaginings." I was in a restaurant with a friend who spilled something on her dress. She was sure it would leave a stain. I said, "We will give it a treatment: *Evil is unreal and leaves no stain.*" There was never the slightest stain left on the dress. You couldn't tell where the accident had happened. In the fourth dimension, evil has never been registered. It is only in your mind that man experiences loss, lack, failure, sickness, sorrow, etc.

Often people go through life resenting and disliking some particular person, thereby keeping the unhappy situation alive and harmful to mind, body, and affairs. A woman came to me full of resentment toward her niece. Whatever her niece did irritated her. She said, "All I can think about is how badly my niece cleans her silver." It seemed a trivial matter, but it was reacting on her in the form of rheumatism. I said, "Send her love and goodwill, and don't give her any advice. Let Infinite Wisdom illumine and direct her." Much to her surprise, her niece gave the silver a wonderful shine and changed in many ways.

You will obtain magic results when you really give this Supreme Intelligence the right of way. *The tide has turned to stay, for God has right of way.* I gave this affirmation when I was speaking in California. A man in the audience came to me after the meeting and said, "That is a marvelous affirmation. I am an engineer, and I know what it means to have the right of way."

Desire is a tremendous power and must be rightly directed. You may desire the wrong things and conditions, so to give the Supreme Intelligence right of *you,* you must say, *I desire only that which God desires through me.* The wrong desire will fade out and be replaced by the right aspirations. As you look back, you will say, "Thank heaven I didn't get the things I desired so much when I was 18," or "I wish I hadn't gotten the things I wanted at 22." You make sure your wishes are foolproof by saying, *I desire the Divine ideas only to come to pass, under grace and in perfect ways.*

I say in *The Game of Life and How to Play It* that health, wealth, love, and perfect self-expression are the square of life. See ye first the fourth dimension, and the perfect plan of your life will come to pass. You will fill the place that you can fill and no one else can fill. Righteous desires of the heart, no matter how extravagant or seemingly unattainable, will be added unto you.

"Ask, and it shall be given you; seek, and ye shall find; knock, and it shall be opened unto you."

— MATTHEW 7:7

✢ ✢

ABOUT THE AUTHOR

Florence Scovel Shinn was born in 1871 in Camden, New Jersey. She was a gifted teacher, artist, and writer who shaped the fields of spiritual growth and New Thought. Through her inspiring work and numerous books, she was a profound influence on best-selling author and metaphysical lecturer and teacher Louise Hay, as well as many other pioneers of personal transformation.

✝ ✝

NOTES

NOTES

Hay House Titles of Related
✷ Interest ✷

YOU CAN HEAL YOUR LIFE, the movie,
starring Louise Hay & Friends
(available as an online streaming video)
www.hayhouse.com/louise-movie

THE SHIFT, the movie,
starring Dr. Wayne W. Dyer
(available as an online streaming video)
www.hayhouse.com/the-shift-movie

✣

EXPERIENCE YOUR GOOD NOW!
Learning to Use Affirmations, by Louise Hay

MANIFEST YOUR DESIRES: 365 Ways to Make
Your Dreams a Reality, by Esther and Jerry Hicks
(the Teachings of Abraham®)

TUNE IN: Let Your Intuition Guide You
to Fulfillment and Flow, by Sonia Choquette

WISHES FULFILLED: Mastering the Art of Manifesting,
by Dr. Wayne W. Dyer

All of the above are available at your local bookstore,
or may be ordered by contacting Hay House (see next page).

We hope you enjoyed this Hay House book. If you'd like to receive our online catalog featuring additional information on Hay House books and products, or if you'd like to find out more about the Hay Foundation, please contact:

Hay House, Inc.,
P.O. Box 5100, Carlsbad, CA 92018-5100
(760) 431-7695 or (800) 654-5126
(760) 431-6948 (fax) or (800) 650-5115 (fax)
www.hayhouse.com® • www.hayfoundation.org

✢

Published in Australia by:
Hay House Australia Pty. Ltd.,
18/36 Ralph St., Alexandria NSW 2015
Phone: 612-9669-4299 • *Fax:* 612-9669-4144
www.hayhouse.com.au

Published in the United Kingdom by:
Hay House UK, Ltd.,
The Sixth Floor, Watson House,
54 Baker Street, London W1U 7BU
Phone: +44 (0)20 3927 7290 • *Fax:* 44 (0)20 3927 7291
www.hayhouse.co.uk

Published in India by:
Hay House Publishers India,
Muskaan Complex, Plot No. 3, B-2,
Vasant Kunj, New Delhi 110 070
Phone: 91-11-4176-1620 • *Fax:* 91-11-4176-1630
www.hayhouse.co.in

✢